Béla Bartók

Für Kinder

für zwei Gitarren
bearbeitet von Siegfried Steinkogler

For Children

for two guitars
arranged by Siegfried Steinkogler

Béla Bartók: Für Kinder
für zwei Gitarren bearbeitet von Siegfried Steinkogler

UE 37209
ISMN 979-0-008-08847-6
UPC 8-03452-07229-4
ISBN 978-3-7024-7518-5

© Copyright 2017 by Universal Edition A.G., Wien

Inhalt • Contents
Table des matières

1. Allegro 2
2. Andante 3
3. Variationen • Variations 4
4. Rundtanz • Round Dance 6
5. Wehmut • Sorrow 7
6. Tanz • Dance 8
7. Räuberlied • Robber's Song 9
8. Ausgelassenheit • Revelry 10
9. Andante molto rubato 12
10. Dudelsack-Lied (1) • Bagpipe (1) 13
11. Dudelsack-Lied (2) • Bagpipe (2) 14
12. Fangspiel • Game of Tag 16
13. Allegretto 17
14. Spottlied • Teasing Song 18
15. Andante 19
16. Klagelied • Mourning Song 20
17. Romanze • Romance 22

18. Spielende Kinder • Children at Play 23
19. Kinderlied • Children's Song 24
20. Quasi adagio 25
21. Kissentanz • Pillow Dance 26
22. Studie • Study 28
23. Kindertanz • Children's Dance 30
24. Spiel • Play 32
25. Lento 33
26. Allegro 34
27. Ballade • Ballad 36
28. Rundtanz • Round Dance 37
29. Soldatenlied • Soldier's Song 38
30. Allegretto 39
31. Tanzlied • Dance Song 40
32. Allegretto 42
33. Andante sostenuto 43
34. Parlando 44
35. Moderato 45
36. Pentatonisches Lied • Pentatonic Song 46
37. Weihnachtszauberlied • Winter Solstice Song .. 48
38. Allegro non troppo 50

Vorwort

Béla Bartók hat Zeit seines Lebens mit großem Eifer Volkslieder gesammelt. Seine zwischen 1904 und 1936 unternommenen Bildungsreisen – oftmals zusammen mit seinem Komponistenkollegen Zoltán Kodály – führten ihn durch viele ungarische, rumänische, slowakische und andere Regionen bis hin nach Nordafrika und ins entlegene Anatolien. Dabei fertigte er phonographische Aufnahmen an und studierte, sortierte und dokumentierte tausende von Liedern mit minutiöser Genauigkeit. Die hierbei gewonnenen Erkenntnisse hielt er in wissenschaftlichen Abhandlungen fest.

Für den Komponisten Bartók kam die Urkraft der Melodie aus dem Volk, aus der Volksmusik, wie er sie bei den einfachen, nicht akademisch gebildeten Leuten in vielen ländlichen Gegenden kennengelernt hatte. Obwohl der ungarische Meister in seinen Orchester- und Kammermusikwerken nicht auf diese Volkslieder zurückgriff, besitzen doch viele seiner eigenen Melodien in ihrer formalen und strukturellen Klarheit beinahe Volksliedcharakter. In seinem Klavierwerk und seinen Klavierliedern hat Bartók sich hingegen sehr intensiv mit den von ihm zusammengetragenen Volksmelodien auseinandergesetzt. Als herausragendes Beispiel hierfür gelten die bekannten *Rumänischen Volkstänze*, die in zahlreichen Bearbeitungen für diverse Besetzungen existieren.

Die Sammlung von Klavierstücken *Für Kinder* verfasste Bartók in den Jahren 1908/09. Er revidierte sie noch einmal in Amerika im Jahr 1943. Somit darf es als eines der ersten umfangreichen Werke gelten, in denen sich der Komponist systematisch mit Volksliedgut auseinandersetzte, wobei er für den ersten Band ungarische und für den zweiten slowakische Lieder auswählte.

Auf den ersten Blick erscheint das Werk wie eine Sammlung einfach gesetzter Kinderlieder. Bartók bot dem pädagogischen Bereich – Schülern wie Lehrenden – jedoch ein Novum, als dessen herausragende Charakteristika die harmonische Variation sowie das scheinbare Divergieren von Melodie und Begleitung hervorzuheben sind.

Ich selbst habe diese Miniaturwerke erst zu Beginn meines Studiums in einer Fassung für Gitarre solo kennengelernt und dabei – unbewusst – viel in Bezug auf Melodie und Harmonisierung gelernt. Mit der Bearbeitung von *Für Kinder* für Gitarre solo wurde das Gitarrenrepertoire um gehaltvolle Musik eines anerkannten Meisters bereichert. Allerdings hatte die Wahl der Besetzung den Verlust der erklärten Zielgruppe zur Folge, da diese Stücke für junge Gitarristinnen und Gitarristen – also für den Anfängerunterricht – mit erheblichen spieltechnischen Schwierigkeiten verbunden waren.

Das Konzept der vorliegenden Ausgabe sieht vor, die ausgewählten Musikstücke für Anfänger im Kindesalter möglichst einfach zu gestalten. Bei insgesamt zehn Stücken wird die Melodie ausschließlich in der ersten Lage ausgeführt. Die Nummern 1, 3, 4, 9, 18, 20, 21, 23, 24 und 33 eignen sich demnach besonders gut als Einstieg in die Musik Béla Bartóks. Gitarristinnen und Gitarristen erlernen das Prinzip des Lagenspiels mithilfe von einfachem Spielmaterial und vertiefen und erweitern ihre Kenntnisse sukzessive aufgrund des leicht ansteigenden Schwierigkeitsgrades. Die Einteilung in ungarische und slowakische Volkslieder bedingt eine Verminderung des Schwierigkeitsgrades ab Nummer 18, um dann wieder graduell im spieltechnischen Niveau anzuwachsen.

Die gitarristischen Lösungen und Fingersätze sind so gewählt, dass sie dem Original möglichst nahe kommen. Gebräuchliche Bezeichnungen wie die Ziffer im Kreis für die Saitenangabe oder die römische Zahl für die Position sollten dem Schüler verinnerlicht werden. Auf diese Weise beginnen junge Spielerinnen und Spieler schon bald, in Eigenregie weitere Melodien aus ihrem Heft einzustudieren, wodurch künstlerische Eigenständigkeit und Kreativität entschieden gefördert werden. Die gängige Schreibweise „Ziffer mit waagrechter Linie" wurde in einigen Fällen durch eine Verbalformulierung ersetzt (z. B. „2. Finger bleibt bis Takt 16 liegen"). Um den nötigen Spielfluss und den dramaturgischen Aufbau der Stücke zu garantieren ist es erforderlich, diesbezügliche Spielanweisungen einzuhalten.

Mögen diese Neubearbeitungen passionierten Spielerinnen und Spielern aller Altersgruppen Freude bereiten, und sie darin bestärken, den begonnenen Weg mit positiver Energie fortzusetzen.

Siegfried Steinkogler, Juni 2017

Preface

Béla Bartók was an enthusiastic collector of folk songs all his life. Between 1904 and 1936, he undertook research trips through many regions of Hungary, Romania, Slovakia and as far afield as North Africa and isolated areas of Anatolia – often with his composer colleague Zoltán Kodály. Along the way, he made phonographic recordings of thousands of songs and studied, sorted and documented them with minute precision. He also wrote scientific papers about his findings.

For Bartók the composer, the primal power of melody came from the people, from the folk music that he had come to know among the simple, not formally educated people in many rural areas. The Hungarian master did not use these folk songs in his orchestral and chamber music works, but the formal and structural clarity found in many of his own melodies gives them an almost folk-song character. On the other hand, in his piano works and in his songs with a small instrumentation, voice and piano for example, Bartók engaged very closely with the folk songs he collected. The famous *Romanian Folk Dances* that exist in numerous arrangements for various instrumental groupings are an outstanding example.

Bartók wrote the collection of piano pieces *For Children* in 1908/09. He revised them in America in 1943. It is thus one of the first large works in which the composer systematically worked with folk-song material. For the first volume he chose Hungarian songs and for the second, Slovakian.

Superficially, the work appears to be a collection of simply arranged children's songs. But Bartók was offering something new to the music education sector — both students and teachers — with the harmonic variation and the apparent divergence between melody and accompaniment deserving particular mention.

I became acquainted with a solo guitar version of these miniatures at the very beginning of my studies and, inadvertently, learnt a lot about melody and harmonisation. The solo guitar arrangement of *For Children* adds rewarding music by a famous master to the guitar repertoire. The choice of instrumentation meant, however, losing the target group, because these pieces are too technically demanding for young and beginning guitarists.

The aim of the present edition is to present the selected pieces as simply as possible for young beginners. In ten pieces, the melody is played exclusively in first position. Numbers 1, 3, 4, 9, 18, 20, 21, 23, 24 and 33 are particularly suitable as entry points to the music of Béla Bartók. Simple material helps guitarists learn the principle of position playing while gradually deepening their skills thanks to the gently increasing level of difficulty. The division into Hungarian and Slovakian folk songs results in a lower level of difficulty beginning with number 18, before gradually increasing the technical challenge again.

The selected solutions and fingerings for the guitar are meant to be as true to the original as possible. We also wanted to familiarise students with common notations such as the circled number to indicate the string to be used for the required note and the Roman numeral indicating the position. This encourages young players early on to independently practise other melodies from the book, which boosts their artistic autonomy and creativity. In some cases, the common notation 'numeral with horizontal line' was replaced by verbal instructions (e.g. '2nd finger remains depressed until bar 16'). It is important to adhere to the relevant playing instructions in order to maintain the required musical flow and dramatic build-up of each piece.

I hope that impassioned players of all ages will enjoy these new arrangements and that the music will help them continue their journey with renewed vigour.

Siegfried Steinkogler, June 2017

Préface

Une partie de sa vie, Béla Bartók s'est ardemment consacré à la collecte de chants populaires. Entre 1904 et 1906, ses voyages d'étude – souvent entrepris avec son collègue compositeur Zoltán Kodály – l'ont mené dans de nombreuses régions hongroises, roumaines, slovaques, etc., jusqu'en Afrique du Nord et en Anatolie. Il y a réalisé des enregistrements phonographiques et étudié, noté, répertorié avec une précision minutieuse des milliers de chants. Bartók a également rédigé des traités exposant le résultat de ses travaux.

Pour le compositeur, la force originelle de la mélodie venait du peuple, de la musique populaire, celle qu'il avait apprise auprès de personnes simples et sans formation académique lors de ses pérégrinations dans des contrées rurales. Bien que le grand maître hongrois n'ait pas repris ces sources dans ses œuvres orchestrales et de musique de chambre, la clarté formelle et structurelle de ses propres mélodies leur donne presque un caractère de chant populaire. En revanche, Bartók a très largement utilisé les mélodies populaires qu'il avait collectées dans ses pièces pour piano et pour chant et piano. Parmi les exemples les plus parlants, citons les célèbres *Danses roumaines*, qui existent aujourd'hui dans de multiples arrangements et combinaisons d'instruments.

Bartók a composé le recueil de pièces pour piano *Pour les enfants* en 1908–1909. Il l'a révisé en 1943, alors qu'il se trouvait aux États-Unis. Il s'agit donc d'une des premières œuvres d'ampleur où le compositeur ait systématiquement travaillé à partir de sources populaires : des chants hongrois pour le premier volume, des chants slovaques pour le second.

À première vue, l'œuvre se présente comme une suite de simples chansons pour enfants. Bartók offre cependant aux élèves comme aux enseignants une innovation pédagogique, avec notamment des variations harmoniques et une apparente divergence entre la mélodie et l'accompagnement.

J'ai fait la connaissance de ces miniatures au début de ma formation, dans une version pour guitare seule, et j'ai ainsi beaucoup appris – inconsciemment – sur la mélodie et l'harmonisation. L'arrangement de *Pour les enfants* pour guitare seule a enrichi le répertoire pour guitare d'une œuvre substantielle par un maître reconnu. Cependant, cet arrangement manquait le groupe cible original, car il présentait pour les jeunes guitaristes – et donc pour les débutants – de considérables difficultés techniques.

Le but du présent recueil est de proposer une sélection de pièces dans une version la plus simple possible, pour les rendre accessibles aux enfants. Sur une dizaine de pièces, la mélodie se joue entièrement en première position. Les numéros 1, 3, 4, 9, 18, 20, 21, 23, 24 et 33 offrent ainsi une bonne introduction à la musique de Béla Bartók. Les guitaristes y apprennent le principe des positions à partir de pièces simples, et approfondissent et élargissent peu à peu leurs connaissances à mesure que les pièces gagnent légèrement en difficulté. La division en chants populaires hongrois et slovaques entraîne une diminution de la difficulté à partir du numéro 18, puis le niveau technique augmente à nouveau progressivement.

Les adaptations et doigtés pour la guitare sont étudiés pour rester le plus proche possible de l'original. La partition comporte les notations courantes, comme les chiffres entourés pour la corde ou les chiffres romains pour la position, que l'élève devrait intégrer. Ainsi, les jeunes musiciens sauront bientôt travailler seuls d'autres mélodies du recueil, prise d'initiative qui favorise grandement l'autonomie musicale et la créativité. Dans certains cas, la notation courante « chiffre avec ligne horizontale » est remplacée par une explication (par ex. : « Le 2ᵉ doigt reste posé jusqu'à la mesure 16 »). Pour assurer la fluidité et la progression dramaturgique des pièces, il est nécessaire de respecter ces indications.

J'espère que ces arrangements réjouiront les passionnés de guitare de tous âges, et leur donneront beaucoup d'énergie positive pour poursuivre leur chemin.

Siegfried Steinkogler, juin 2017

1. Allegro

Béla Bartók
(1881–1945)
arr. Siegfried Steinkogler

2. Andante

Béla Bartók
arr. S. Steinkogler

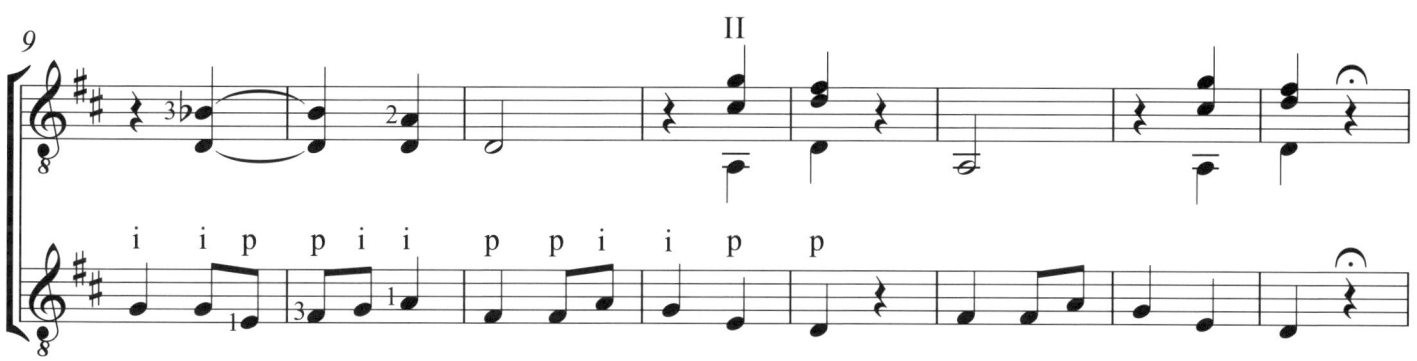

3. Variationen · Variations

Béla Bartók
arr. S. Steinkogler

4. Rundtanz • Round Dance

Béla Bartók
arr. S. Steinkogler

5. Wehmut • Sorrow

Béla Bartók
arr. S. Steinkogler

© Copyright 2017 by Universal Edition A.G., Wien

UE 37 209

6. Tanz • Dance

Béla Bartók
arr. S. Steinkogler

7. Räuberlied • Robber's Song

Béla Bartok
arr. S. Steinkogler

© Copyright 2017 by Universal Edition A.G., Wien

UE 37 209

8. Ausgelassenheit • Revelry

Béla Bartók
arr. S. Steinkogler

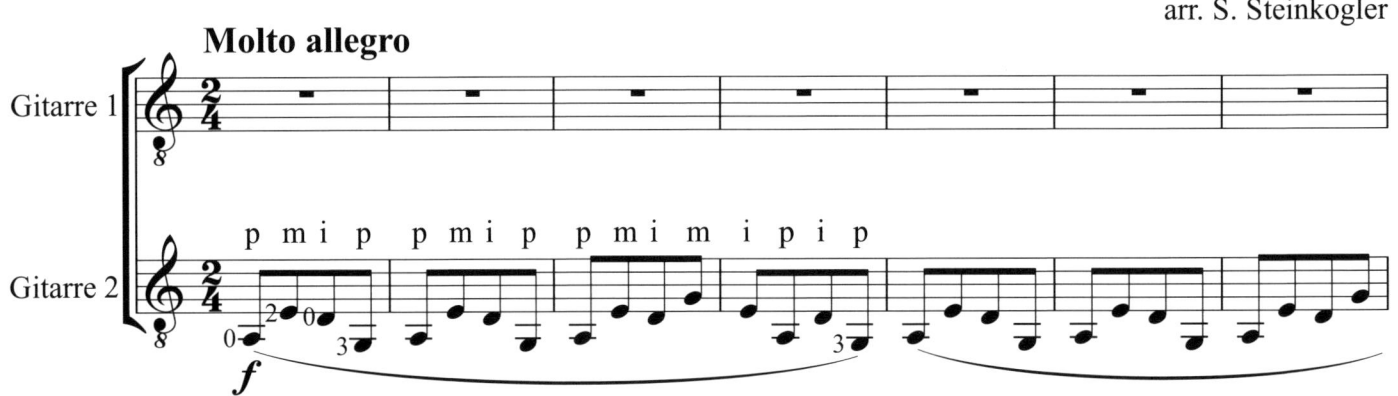
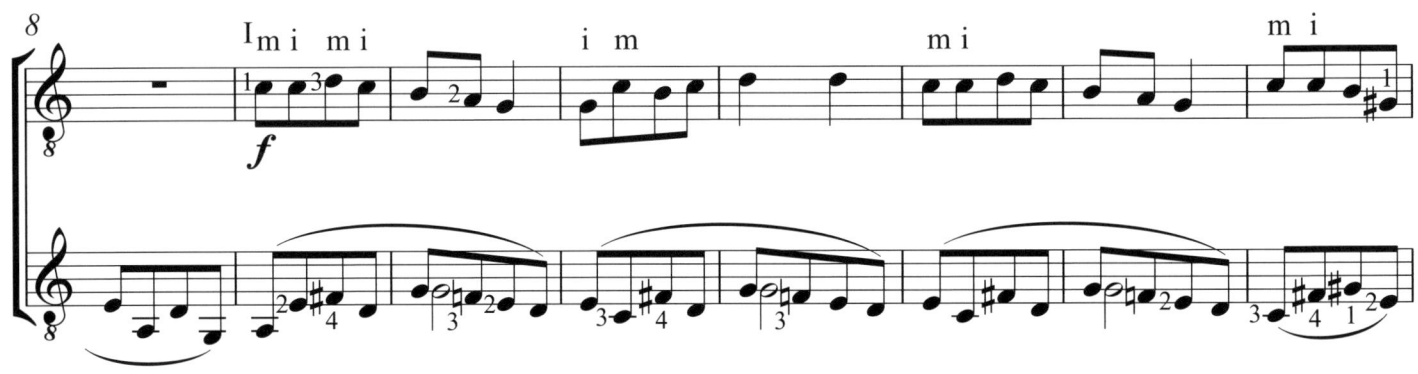
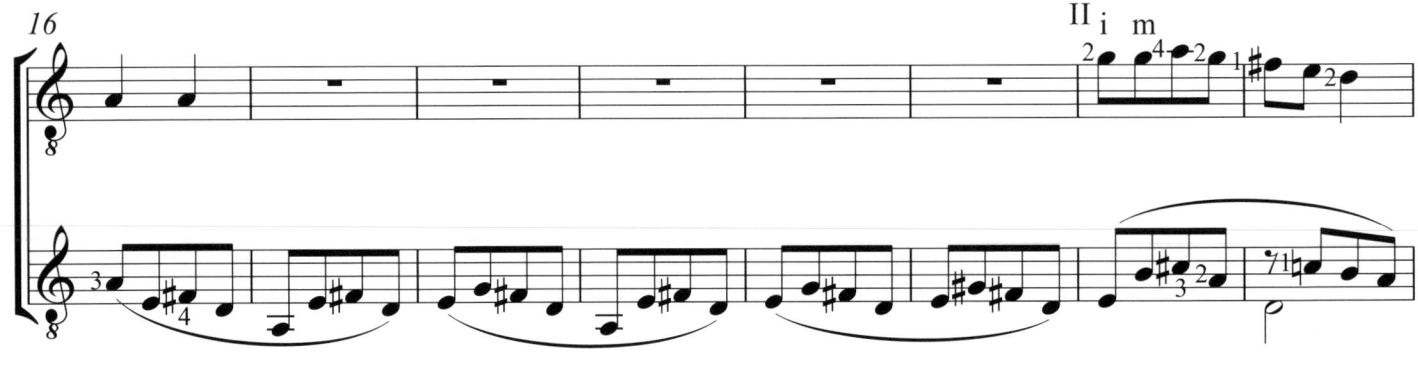

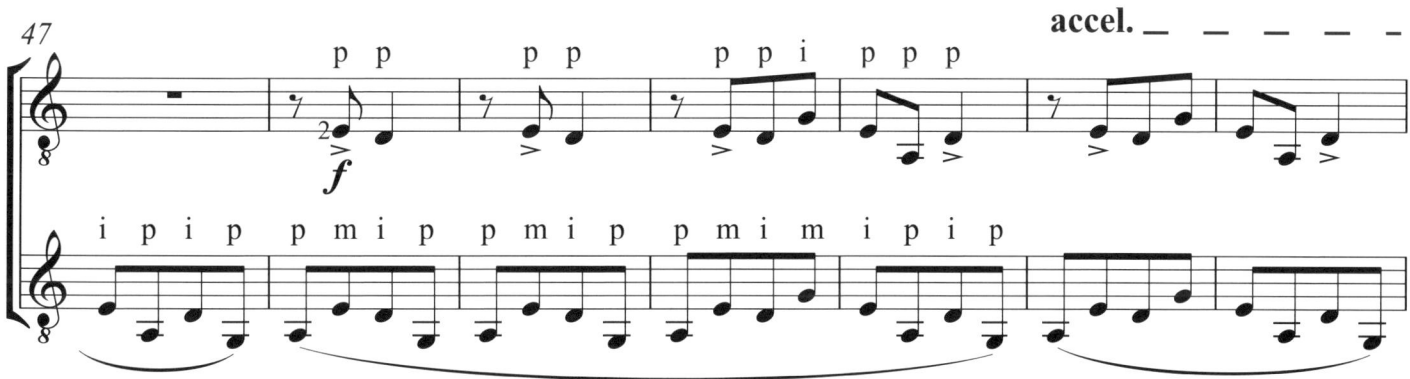
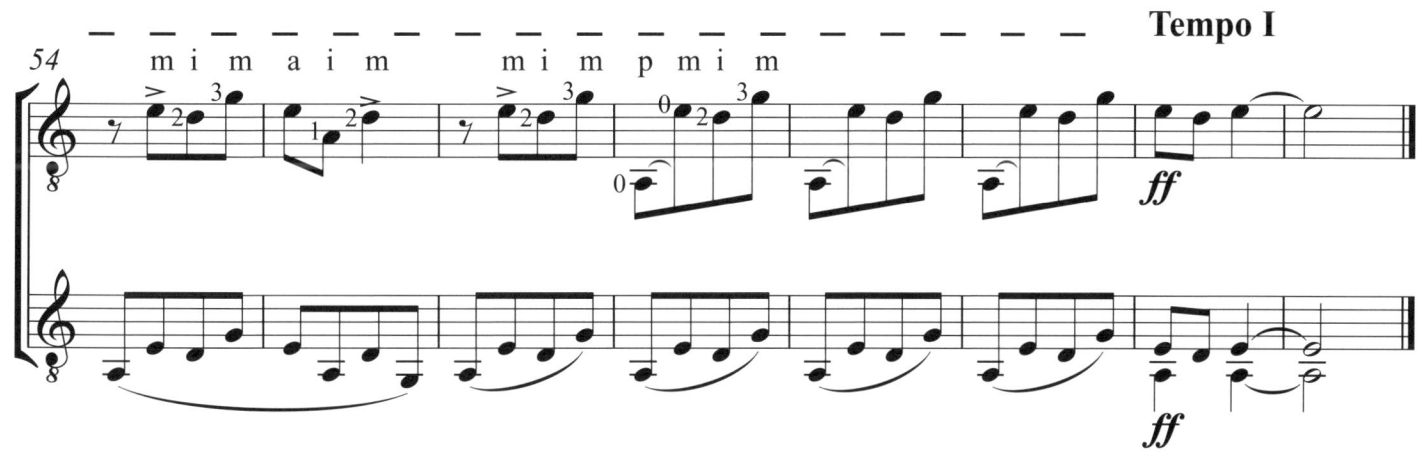

9. Andante molto rubato

Béla Bartók
arr. S. Steinkogler

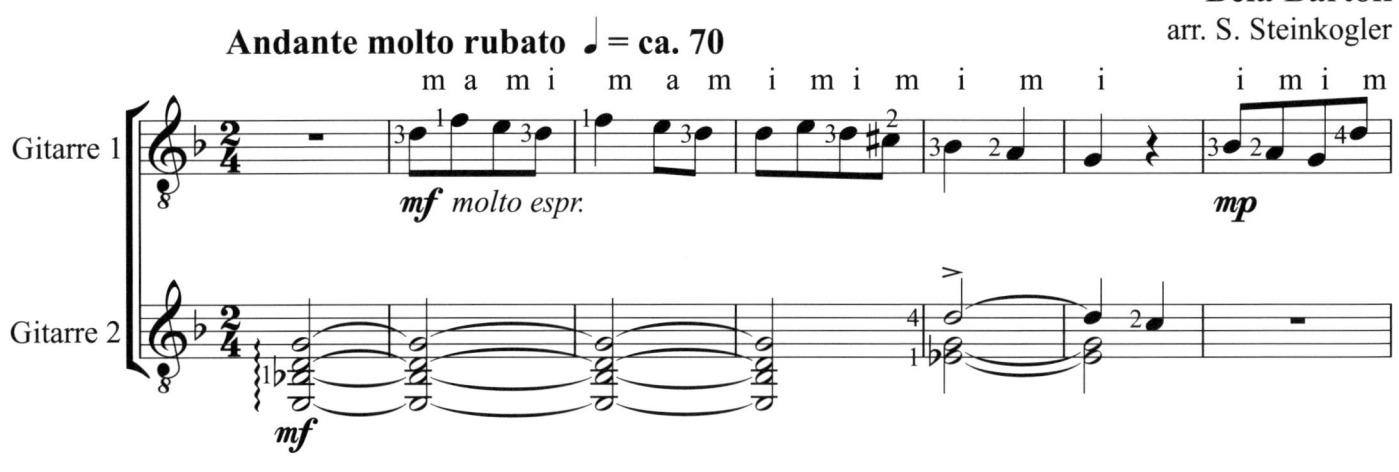

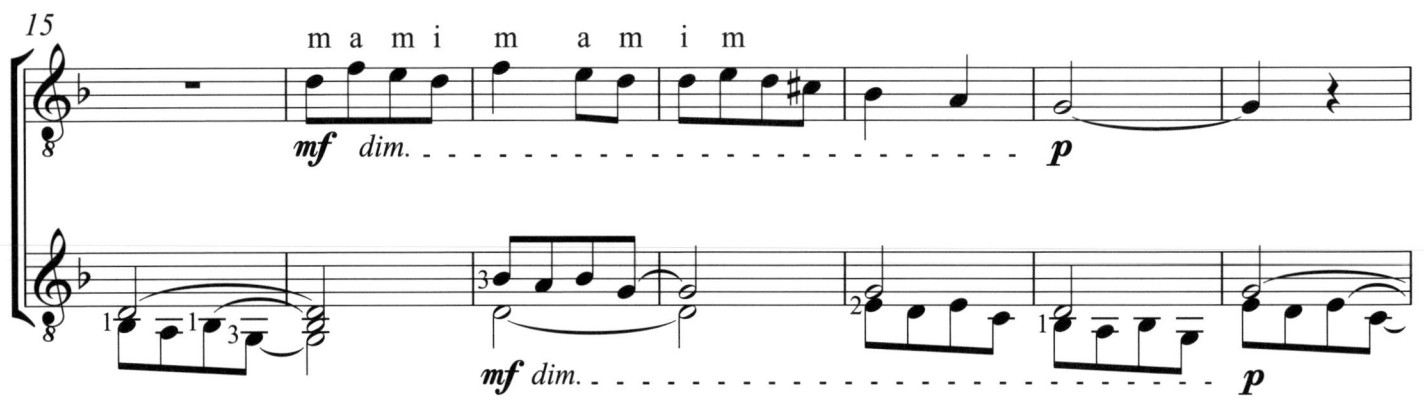

© Copyright 2017 by Universal Edition A.G., Wien

10. Dudelsack-Lied (1) • Bagpipe (1)

Béla Bartók
arr. S. Steinkogler

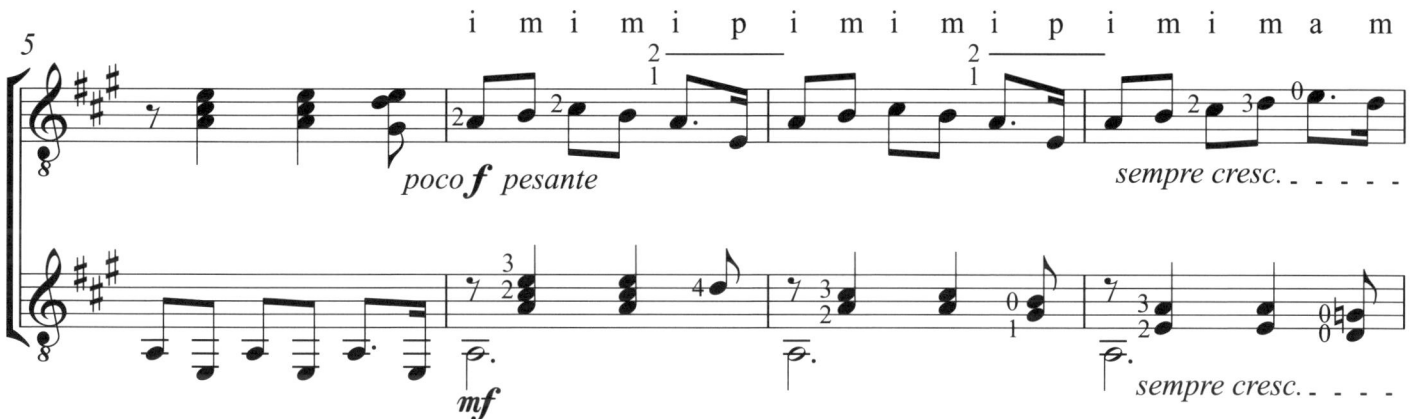

© Copyright 2017 by Universal Edition A.G., Wien

11. Dudelsack-Lied (2) • Bagpipe (2)

Béla Bartók
arr. S. Steinkogler

12. Fangspiel • Game of Tag

Béla Bartók
arr. S. Steinkogler

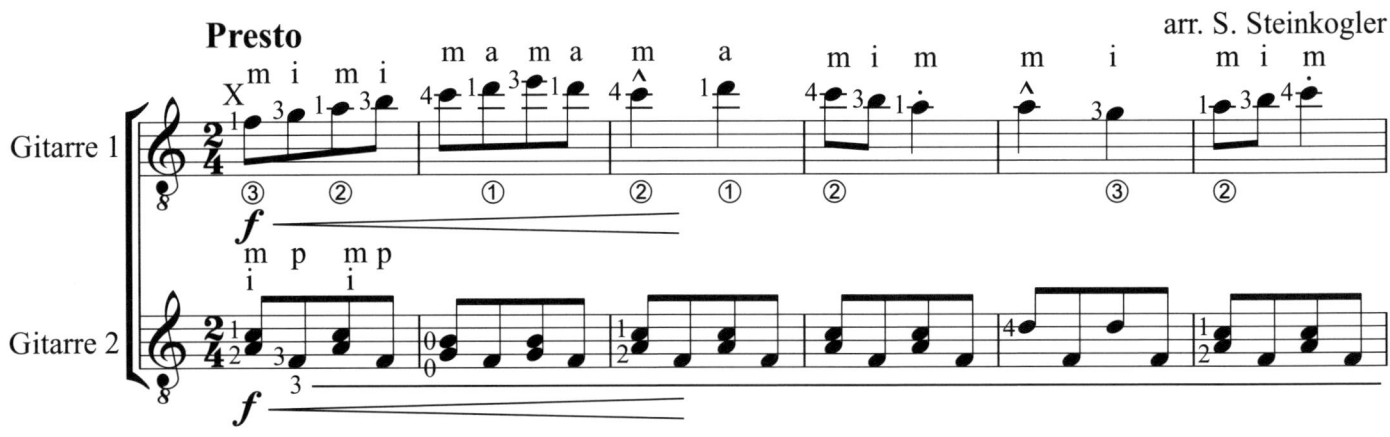

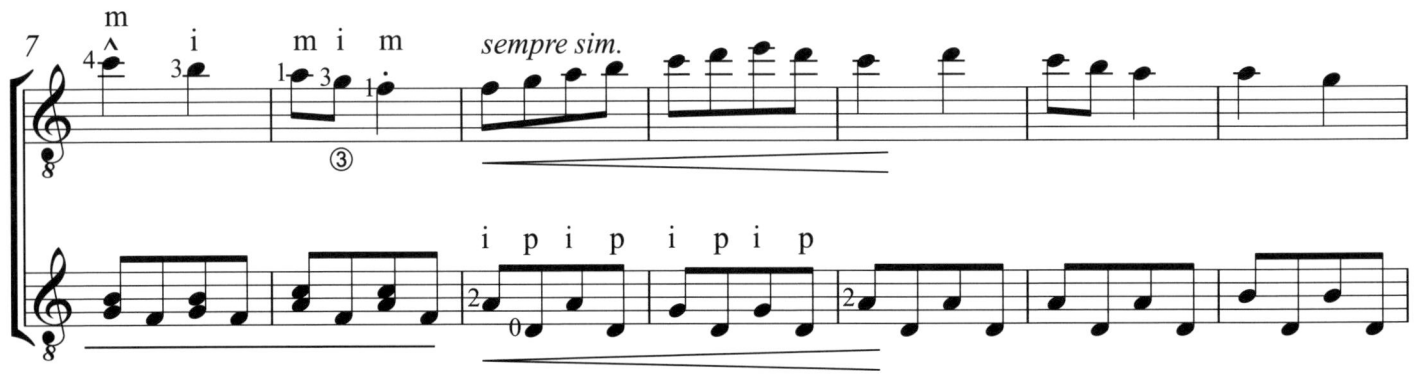

© Copyright 2017 by Universal Edition A.G., Wien

UE 37 209

13. Allegretto

Béla Bartók
arr. S. Steinkogler

14. Spottlied · Teasing Song

Béla Bartók
arr. S. Steinkogler

15. Andante

Béla Bartók
arr.: S. Steinkogler

16. Klagelied • Mourning Song

Béla Bartók
arr. S. Steinkogler

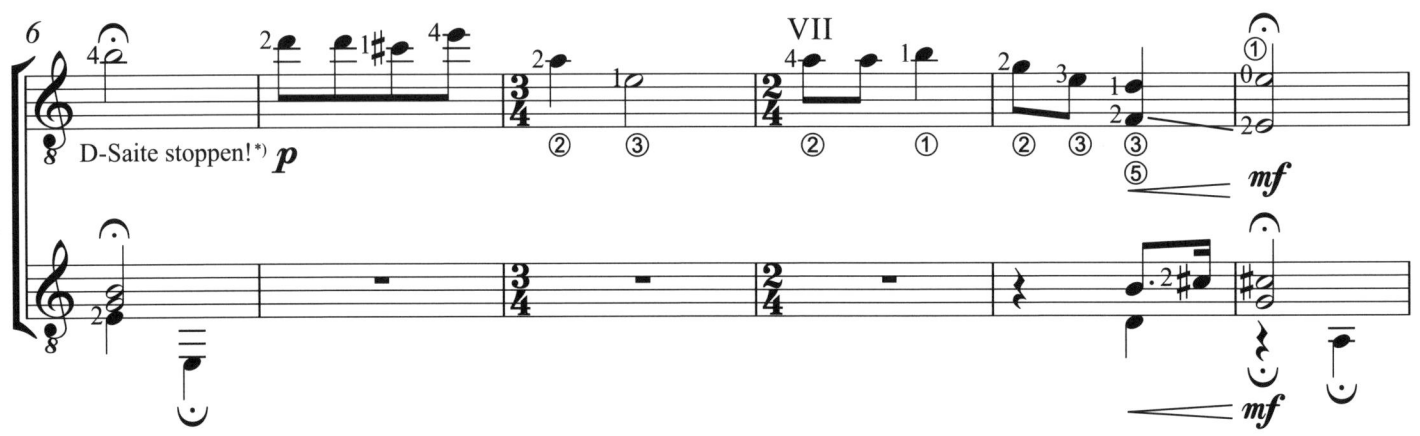

*) Stop D string! • Stopper le ré!

© Copyright 2017 by Universal Edition A.G., Wien

UE 37 209

17. Romanze · Romance

Béla Bartók
arr. S. Steinkogler

18. Spielende Kinder • Children at Play

Béla Bartók
arr. Siegfried Steinkogler

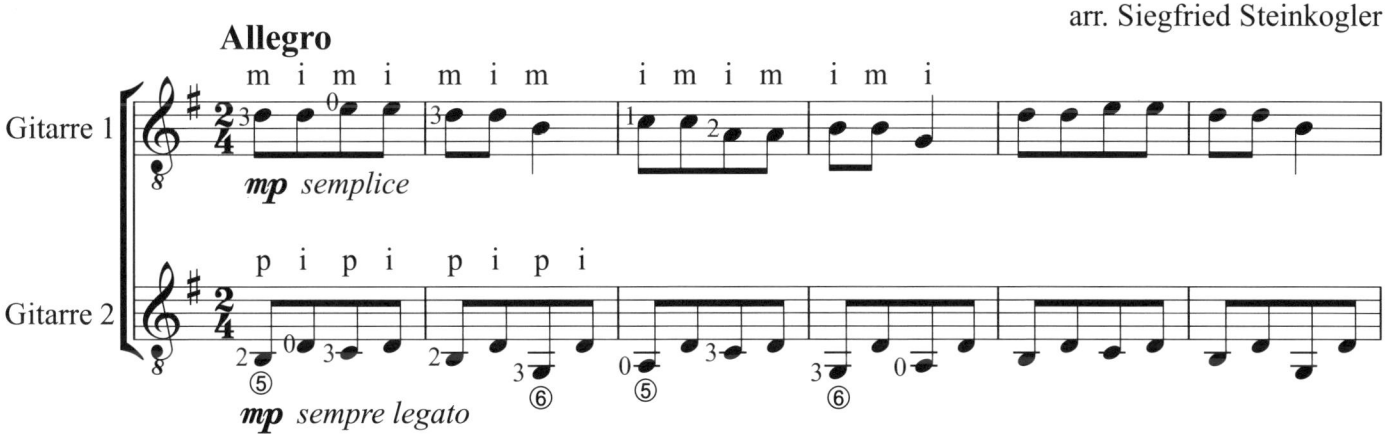
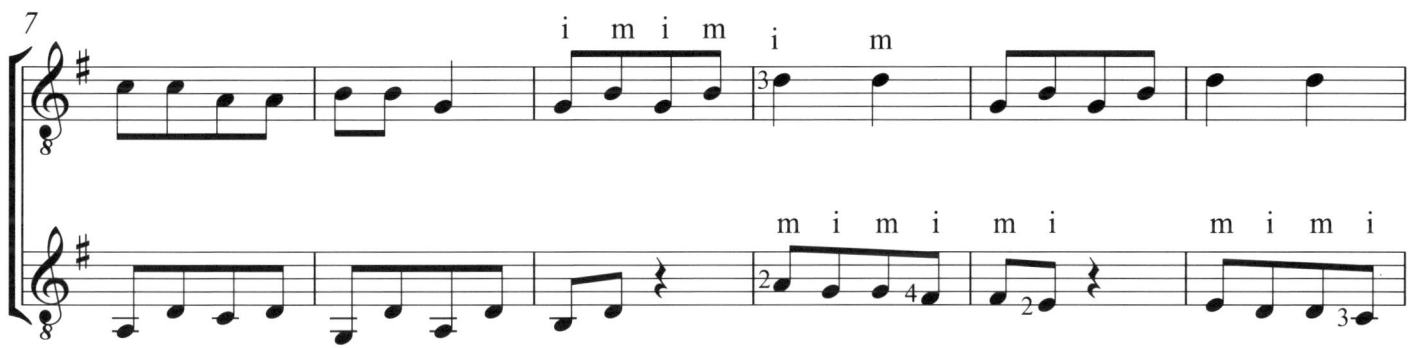
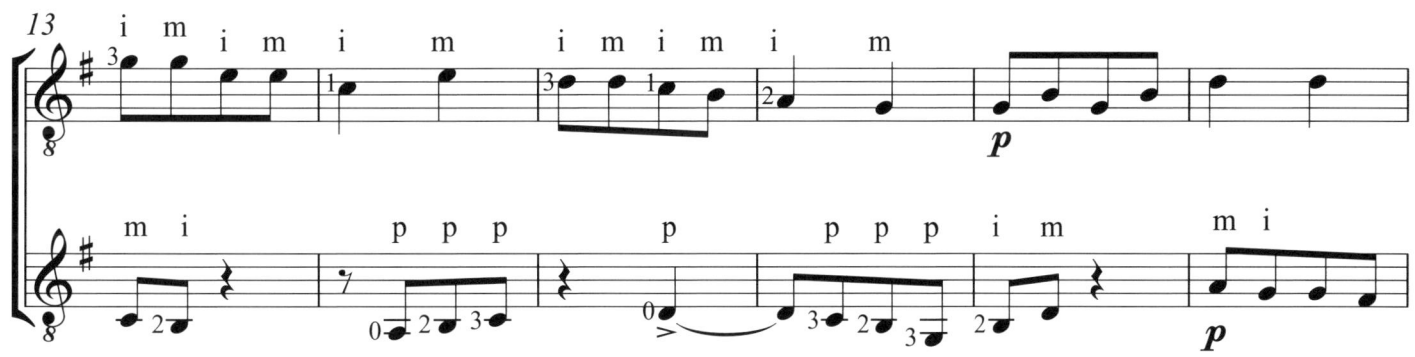

19. Kinderlied • Children's Song

Béla Bartók
arr. S. Steinkogler

© Copyright 2017 by Universal Edition A.G., Wien

UE 37 209

20. Quasi adagio

Béla Bartók
arr. S. Steinkogler

21. Kissentanz • Pillow Dance

Béla Bartók
arr. S. Steinkogler

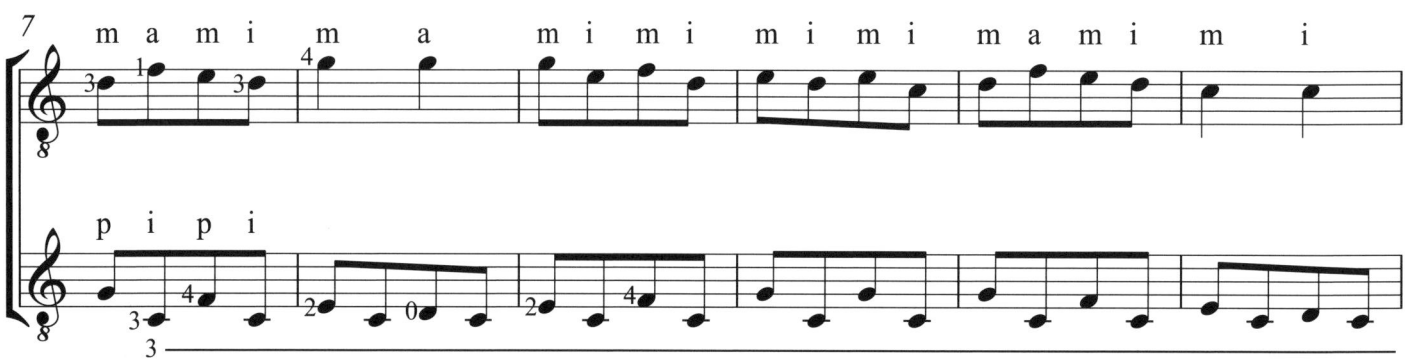

27

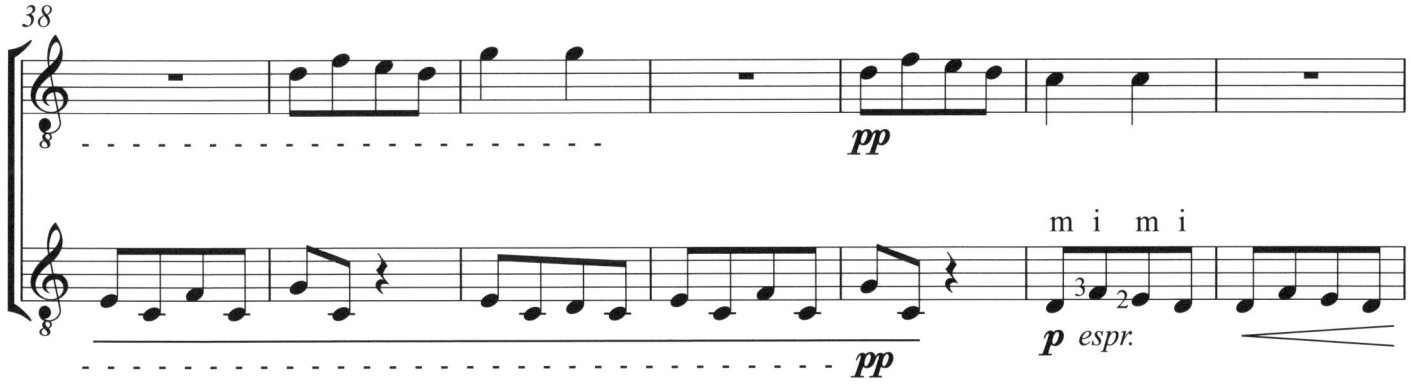
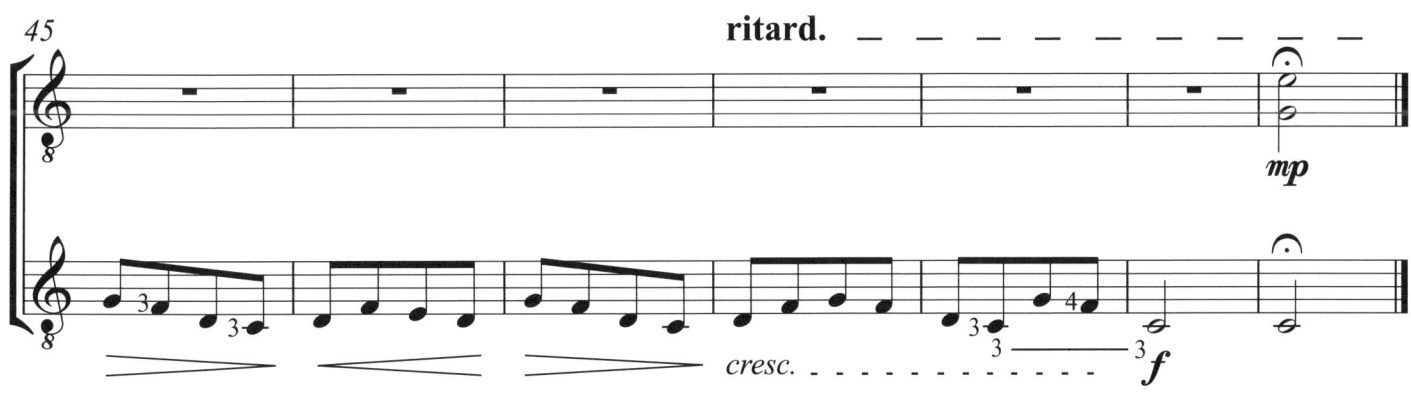

UE 37 209

22. Studie • Study

Béla Bartók
arr. S. Steinkogler

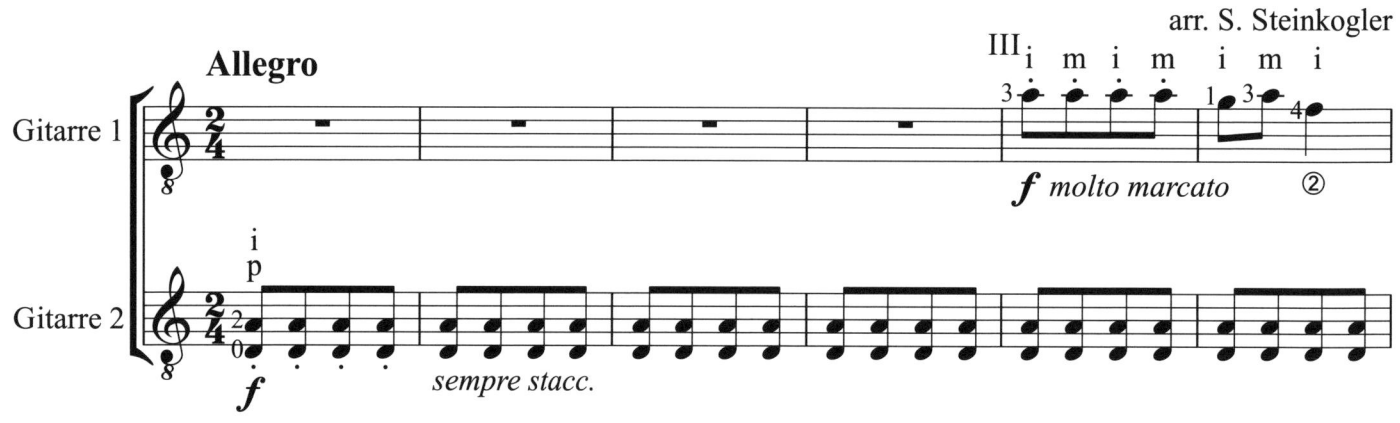

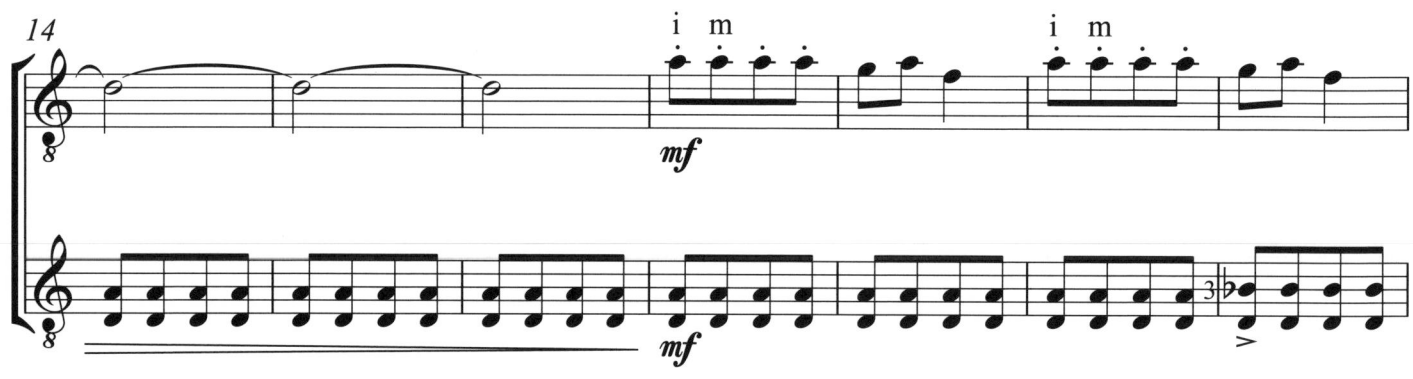

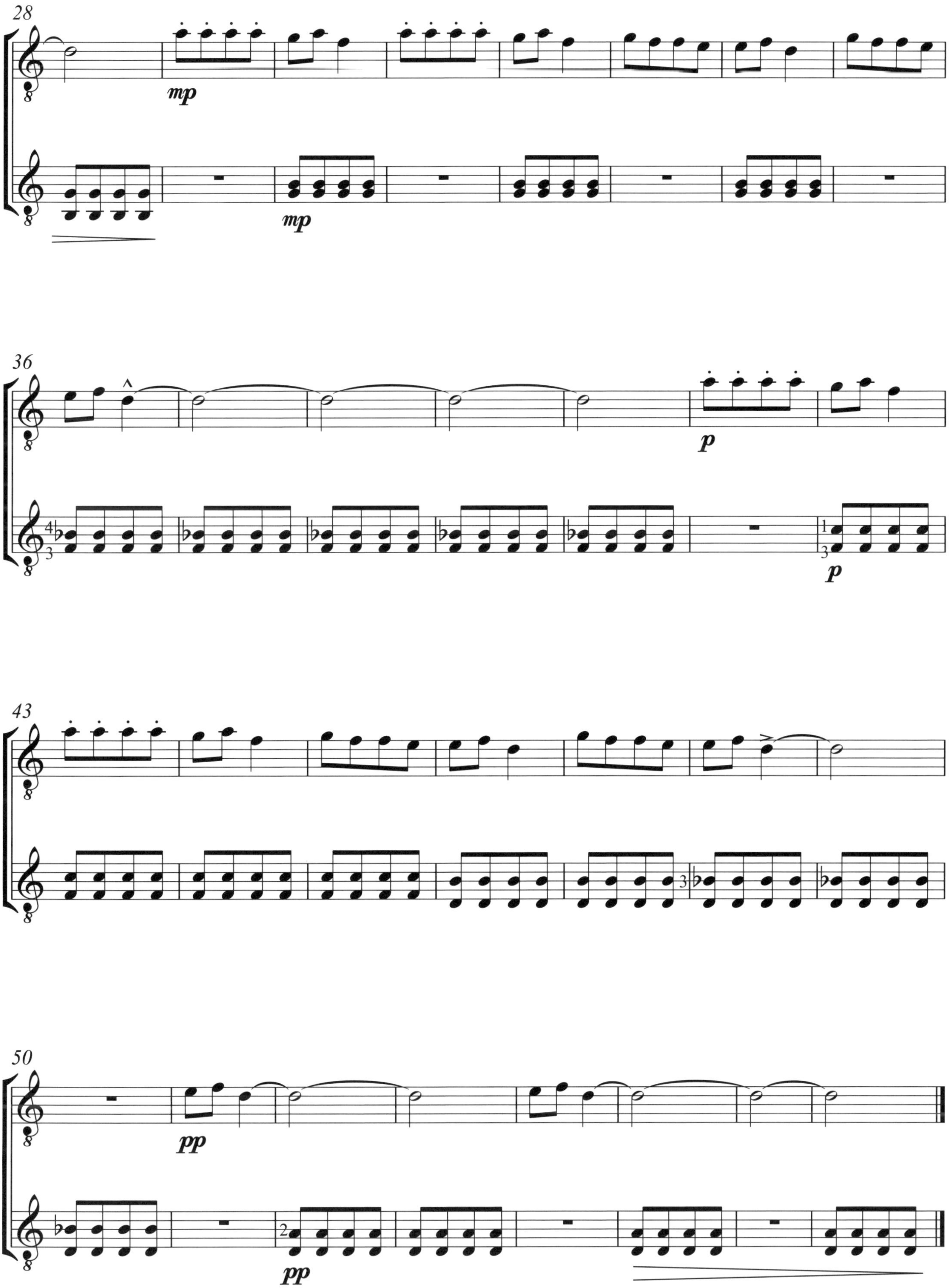
28
mp
mp
36
p
p
43
50
pp
pp

23. Kindertanz • Children's Dance

Béla Bartók
arr. S. Steinkogler

*) 2nd finger remains depressed until bar 16 • Le 2e doigt reste posé jusqu'à la mesure 16

© Copyright 2017 by Universal Edition A.G., Wien

UE 37 209

24
30
mf
f
II
mf
f
36
poco ritard.
a tempo
mf
dim.
IV
mf
f
42
p i m i
f
sff
p i m i
sff

24. Spiel • Play

Béla Bartók
arr. S. Steinkogler

25. Lento

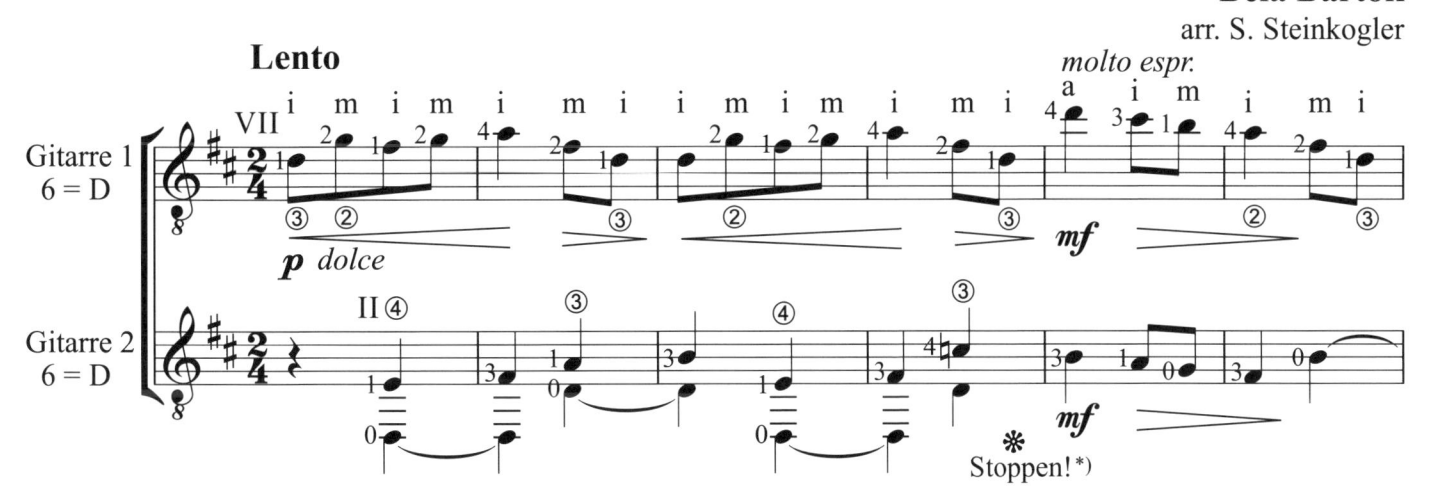

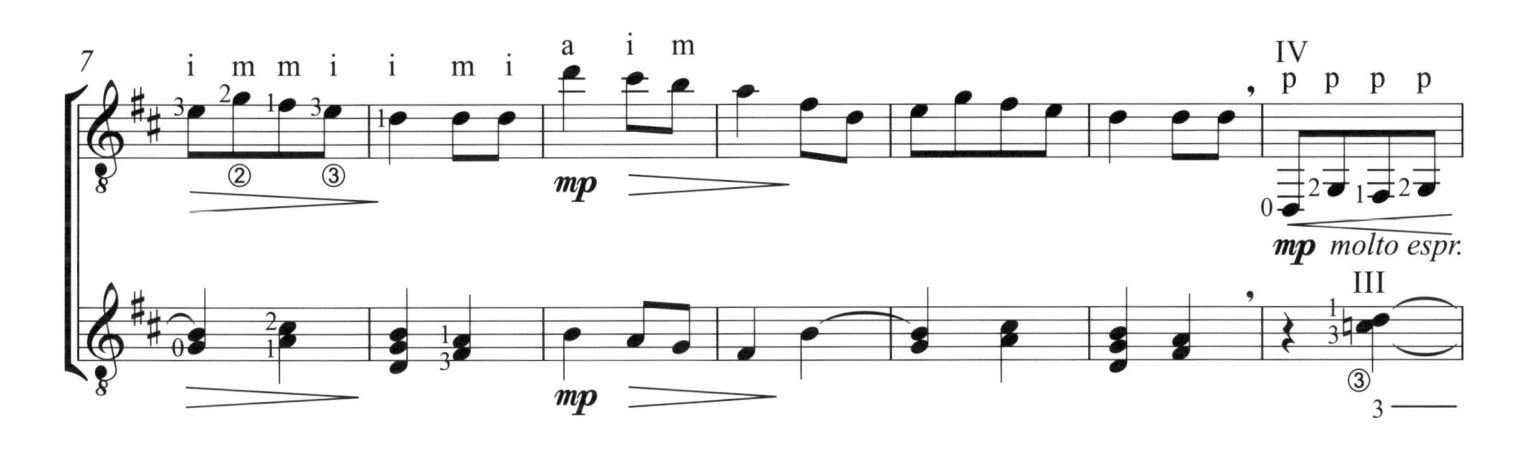

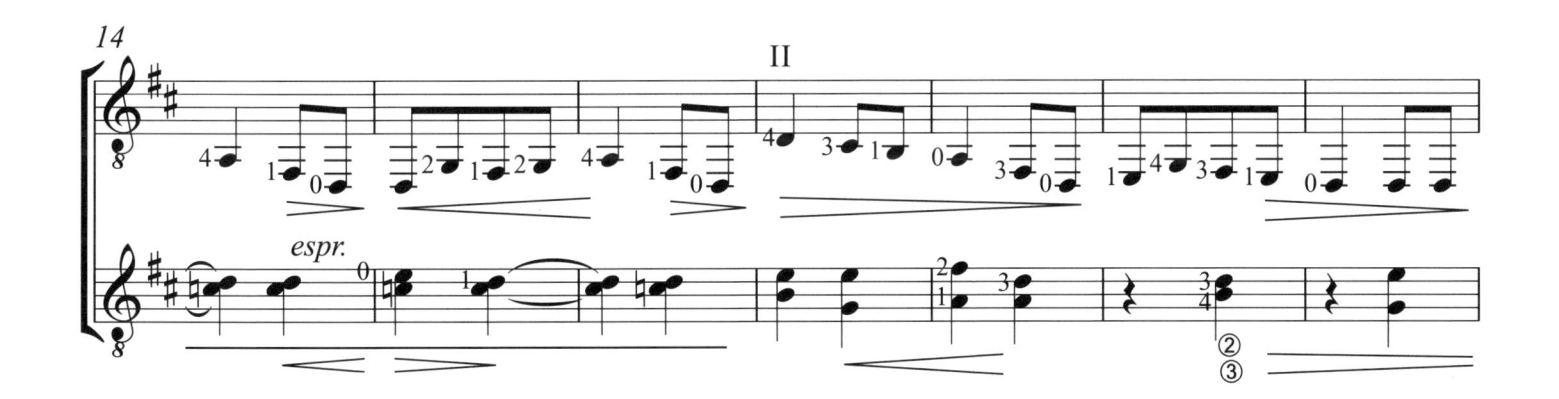

Béla Bartók
arr. S. Steinkogler

*) Stop! • Stopper!

© Copyright 2017 by Universal Edition A.G., Wien

UE 37 209

26. Allegro

Béla Bartók
arr. S. Steinkogler

*) Fingers remain depressed! • Laisser les doigts en place!

© Copyright 2017 by Universal Edition A.G., Wien

UE 37 209

rit. poco
p dolce
a tempo
ritard.
cresc.
a tempo ritard.
p cresc.
mp cresc.

27. Ballade · Ballad

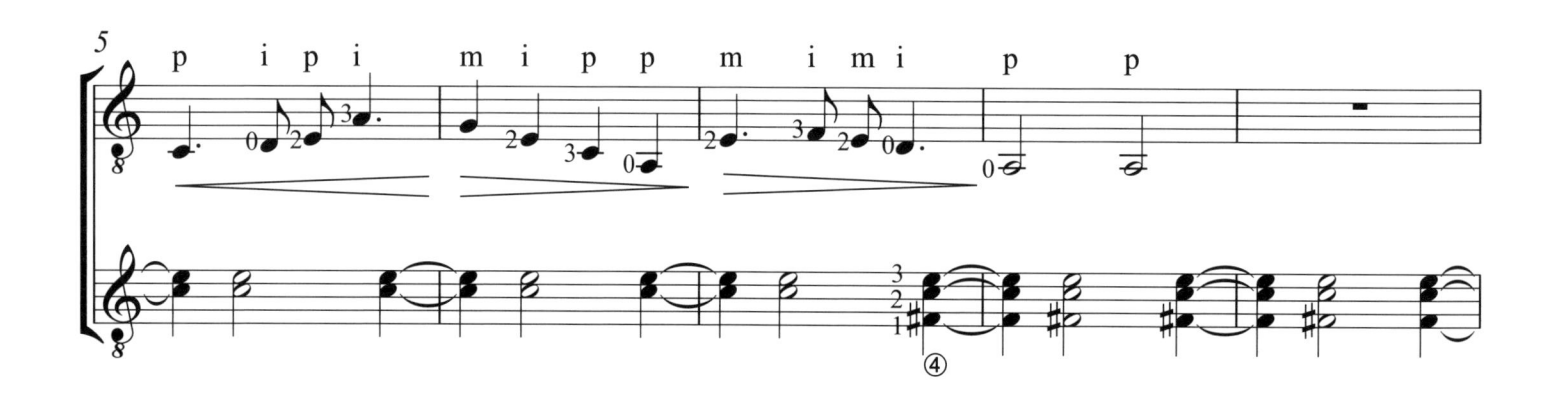

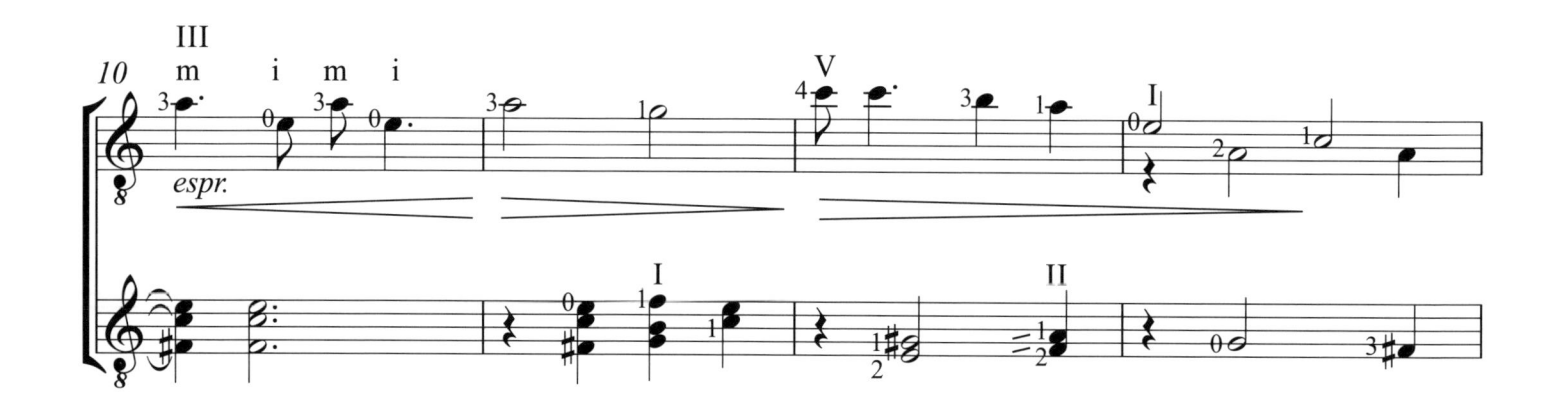

Béla Bartók
arr. S. Steinkogler

28. Rundtanz • Round Dance

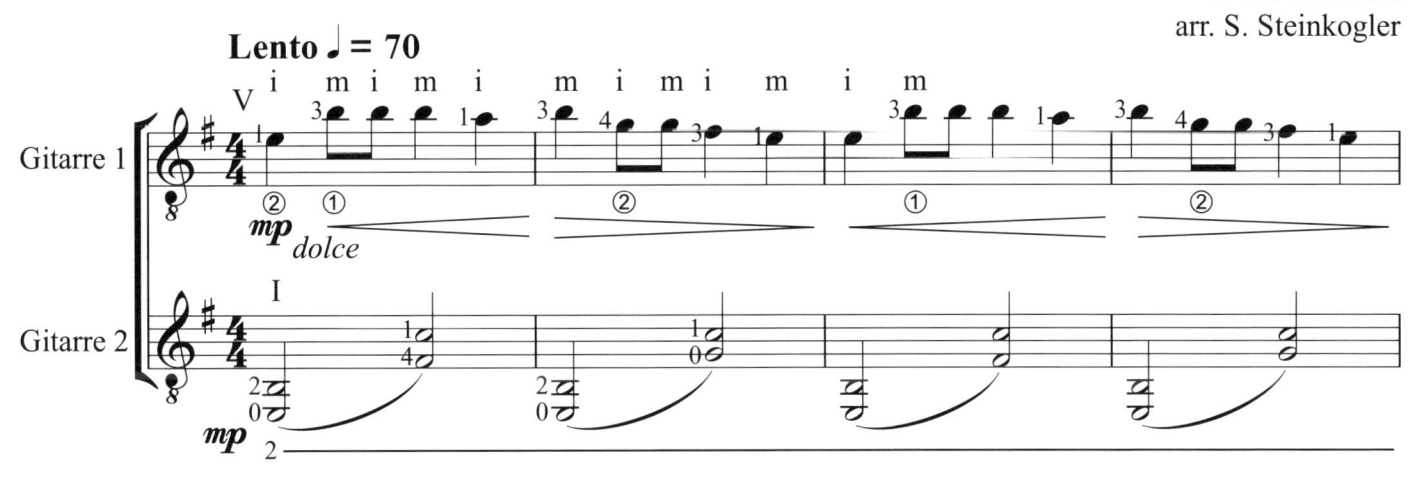

Béla Bartók
arr. S. Steinkogler

29. Soldatenlied · Soldier's Song

Béla Bartók
arr. S. Steinkogler

Andante non troppo ♩ = 100

30. Allegretto

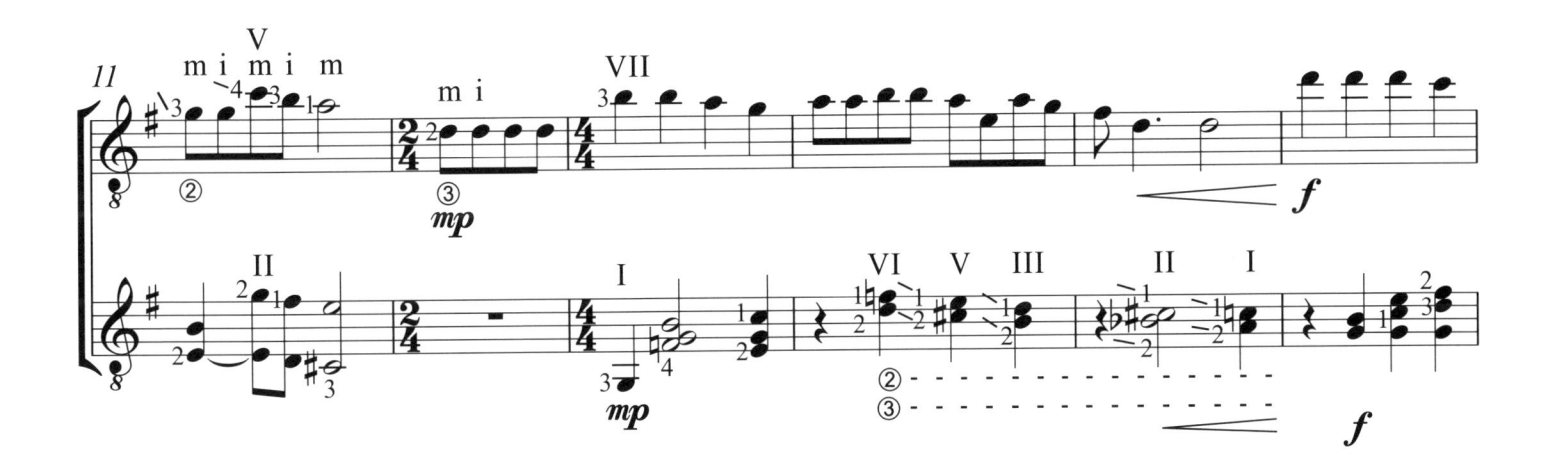

Béla Bartók
arr. S. Steinkogler

31. Tanzlied • Dance Song

Béla Bartók
arr. S. Steinkogler

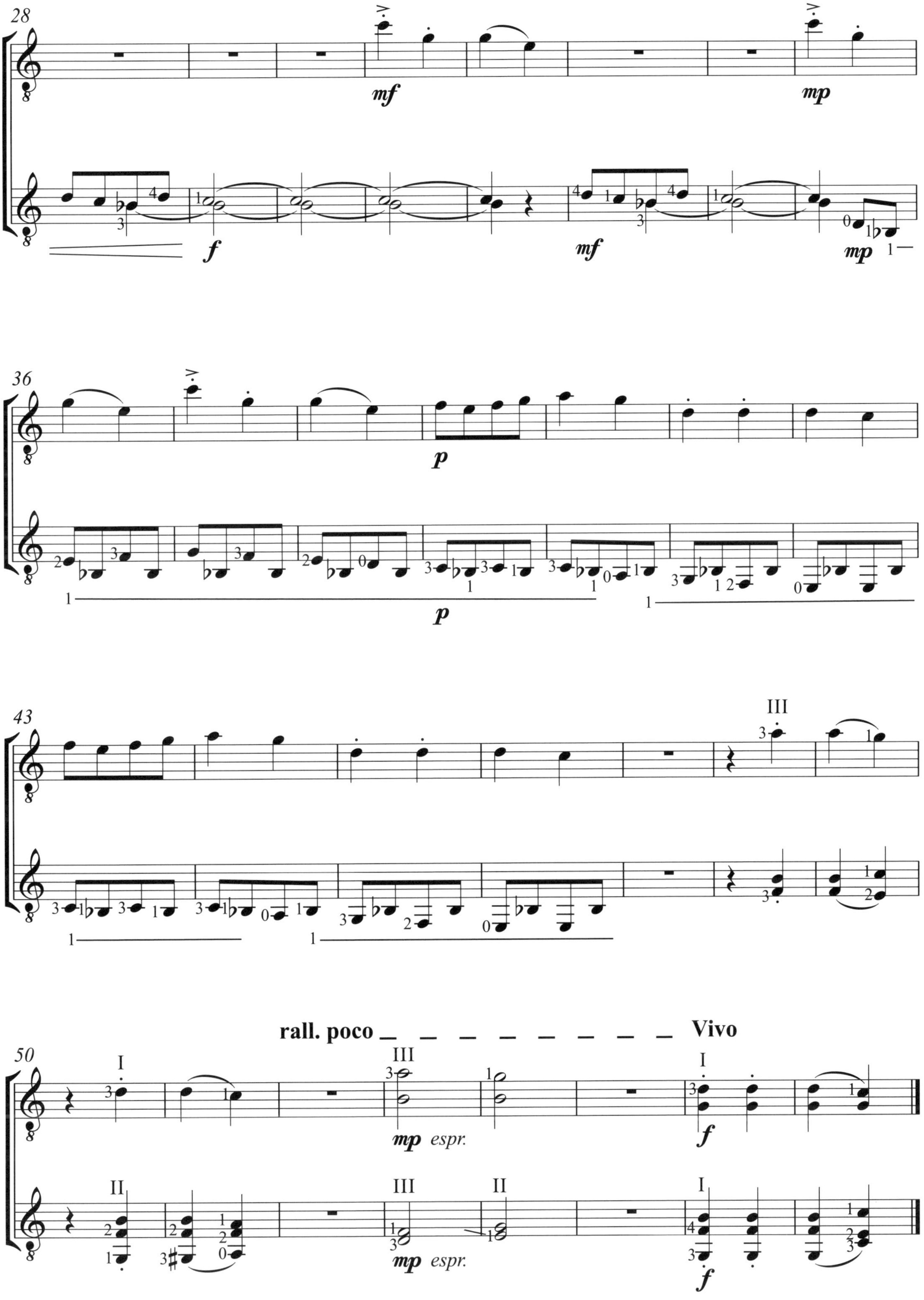
28
mf
mp
f
mf
mp
36
p
p
43
III
rall. poco
Vivo
50
I
III
II
mp espr.
f

32. Allegretto

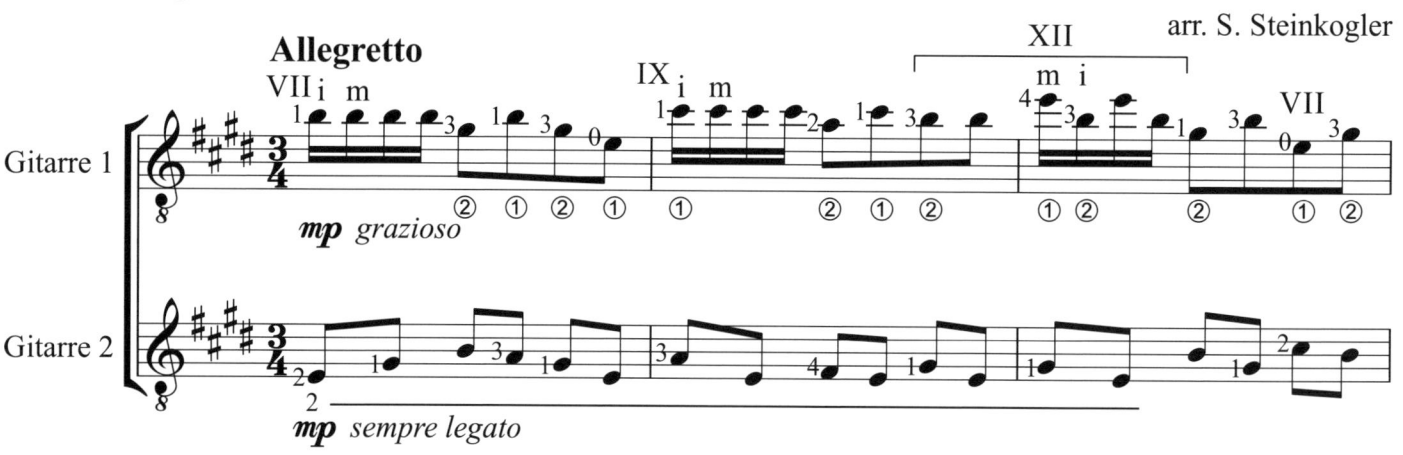

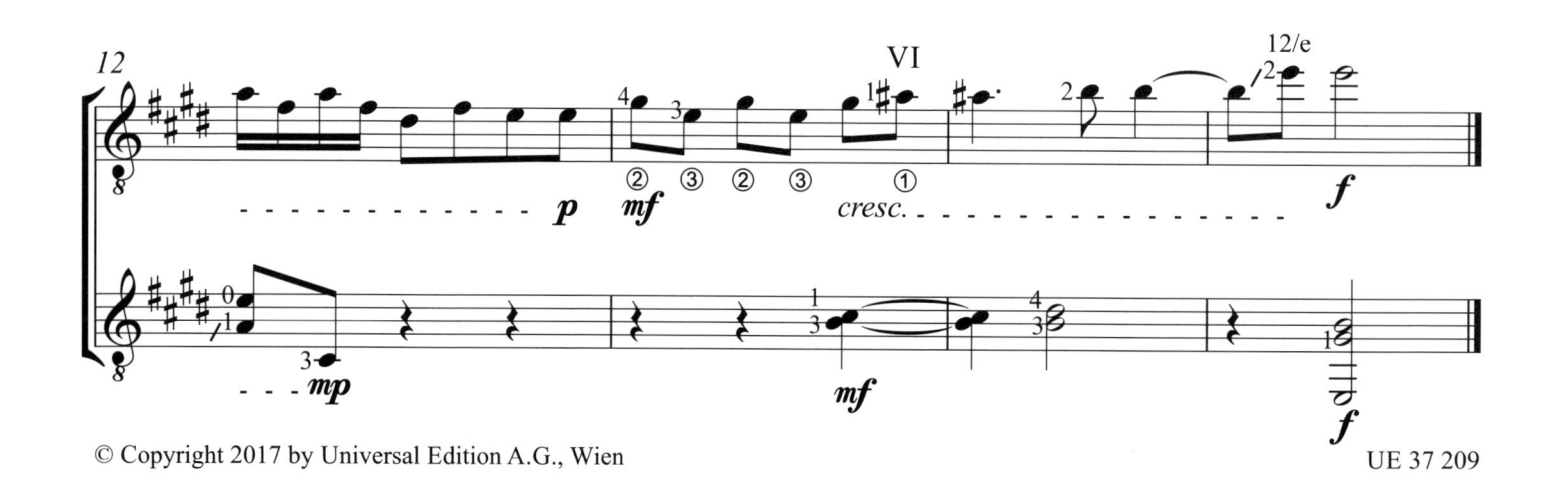

Béla Bartók
arr. S. Steinkogler

33. Andante sostenuto

Béla Bartók
arr. S. Steinkogler

34. Parlando

Béla Bartók
arr. S. Steinkogler

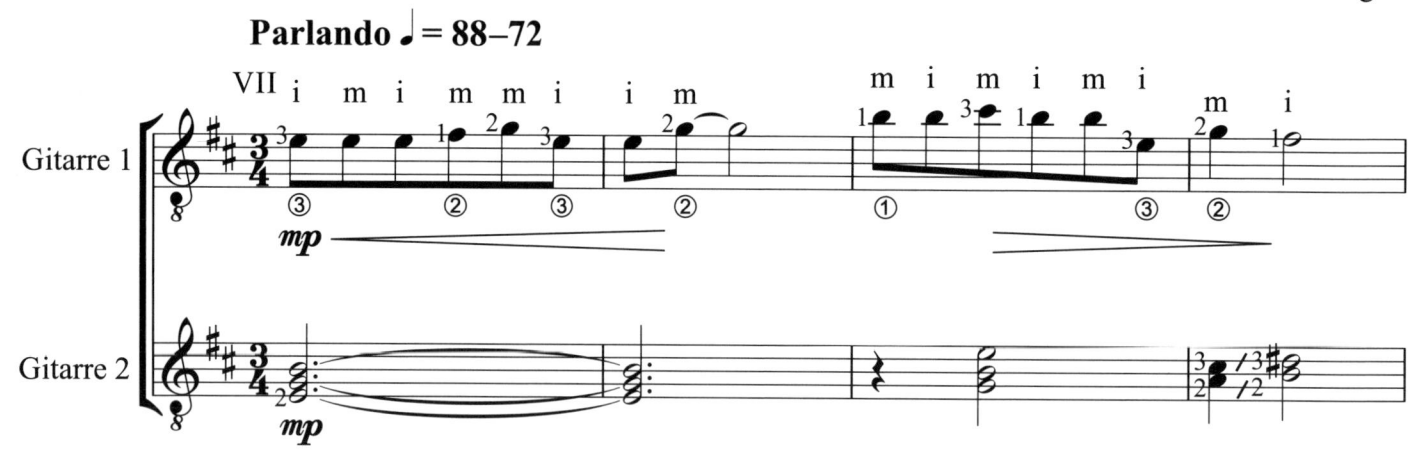

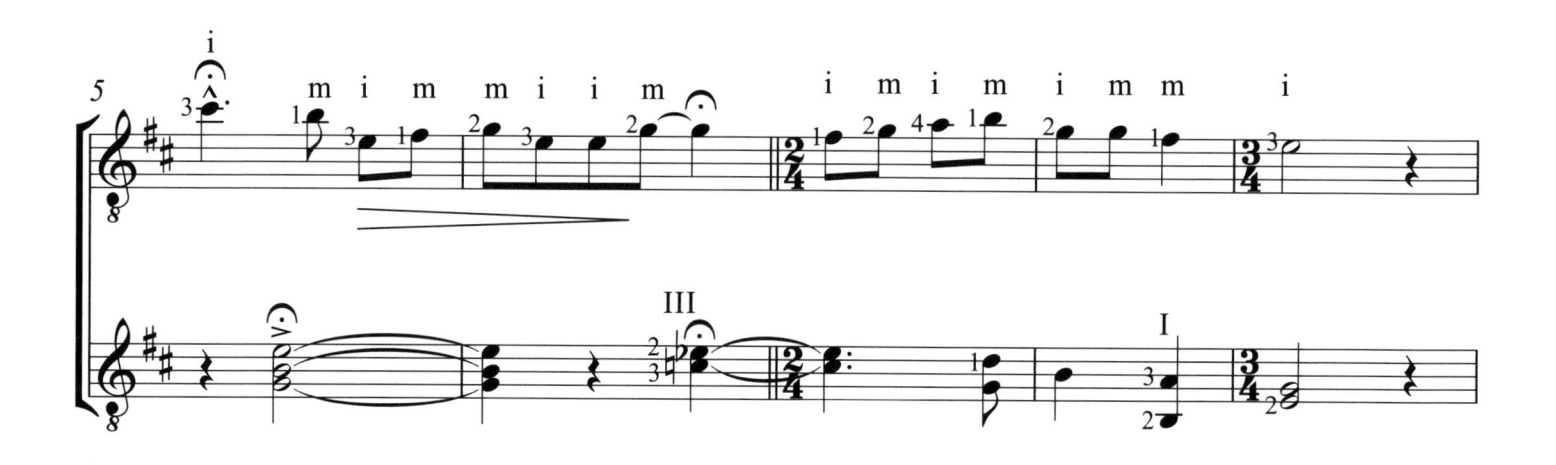

35. Moderato

Béla Bartók
arr. S. Steinkogler

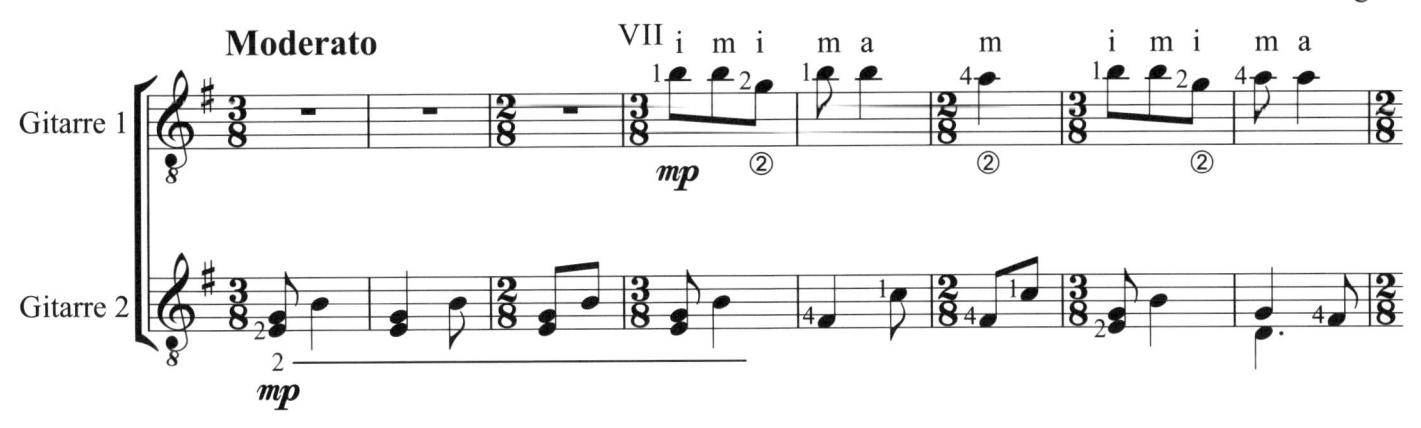

36. Pentatonisches Lied • Pentatonic Tune

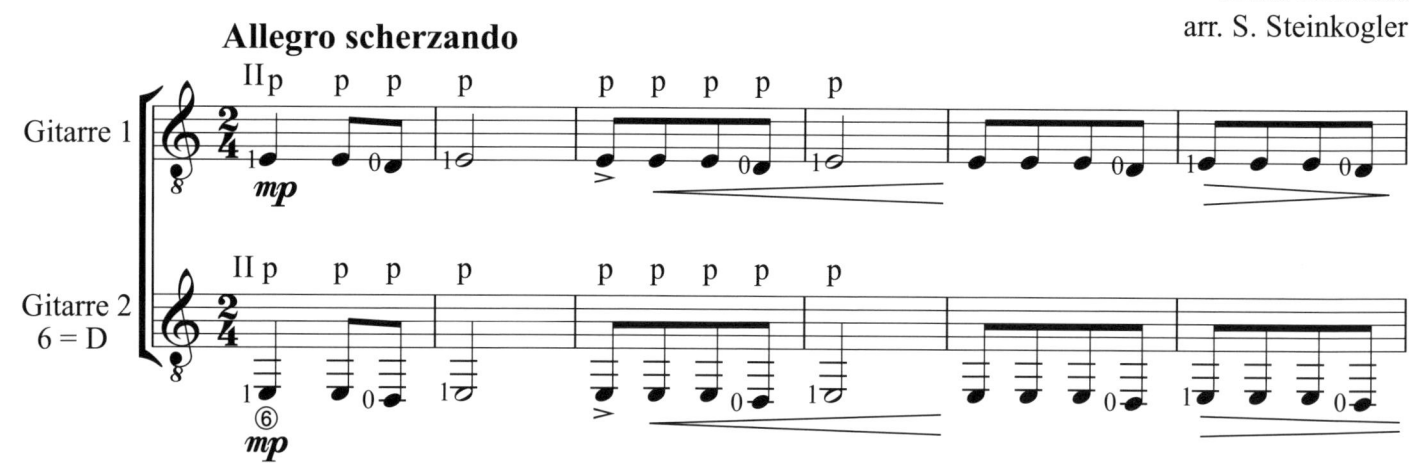

Béla Bartók
arr. S. Steinkogler

*) Stop D! • Stopper le *ré*!

© Copyright 2017 by Universal Edition A.G., Wien

UE 37 209

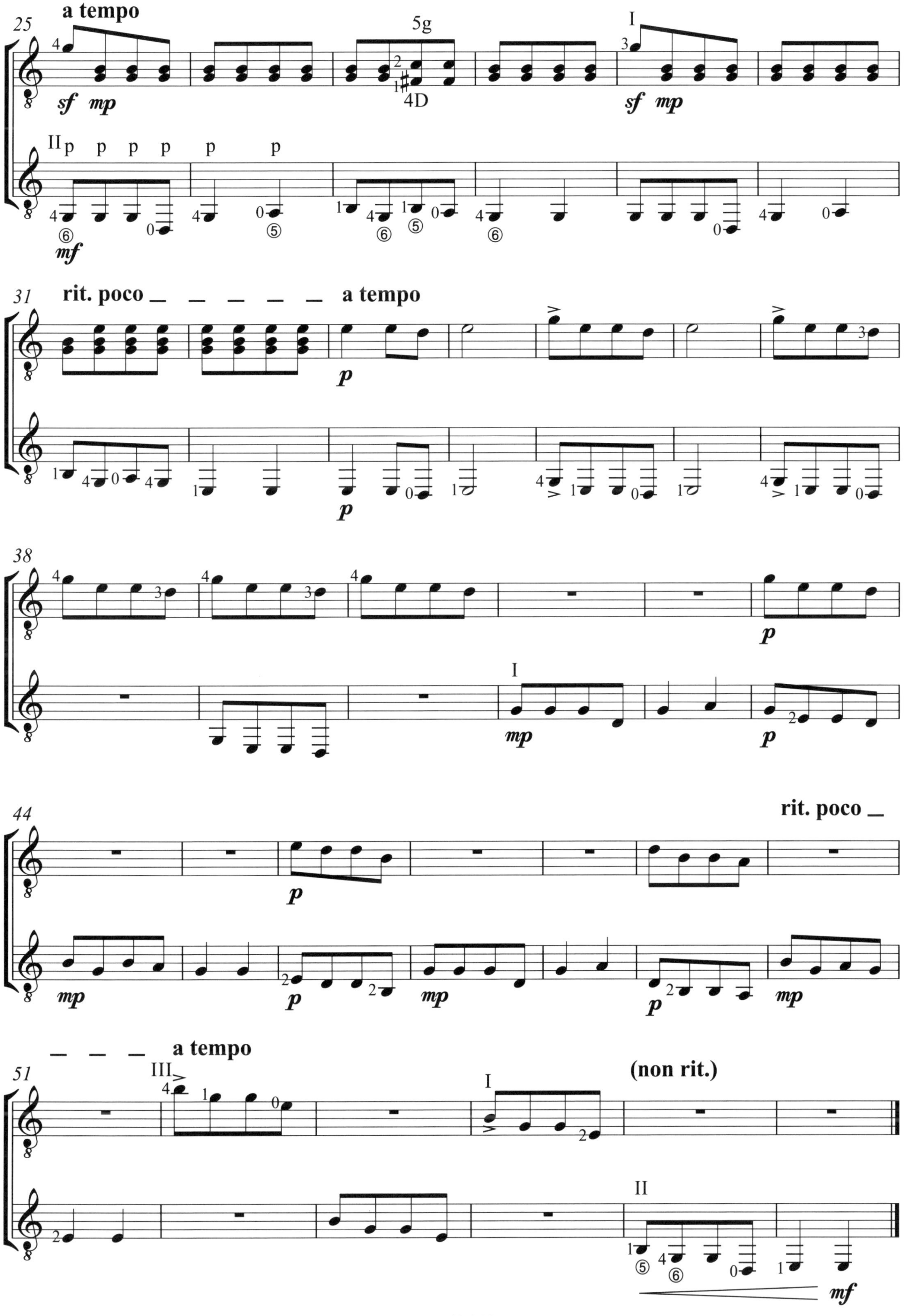
a tempo
rit. poco
a tempo
rit. poco
a tempo
(non rit.)

37. Weihnachtszauberlied • Winter Solstice Song

Béla Bartók
arr. S. Steinkogler

*)   3rd finger remains depressed until bar 20 • Le 3e doigt reste posé jusqu'à la mesure 20
**) 3rd finger remains depressed until bar 18 • Le 3e doigt reste posé jusqu'à la mesure 18
***) 2nd finger remains depressed until bar 44 • Le 2e doigt reste posé jusqu'à la mesure 44
****) 1st and 2nd finger remain depressed until bar 45 • Index et majeur restent posés jusqu'à la mesure 45

© Copyright 2017 by Universal Edition A.G., Wien

UE 37 209

*) 1st finger remains depressed until bar 70 • Le 1e doigt reste posé jusqu'à la mesure 70

UE 37 209

38. Allegro non troppo

Béla Bartók
arr. S. Steinkogler

Weitere Titel für Gitarre • Further titles for the guitar

Siegfried Steinkogler

24 Wettbewerbsstücke • 24 Competition Pieces
Sehr leichte bis mittelschwere Stücke für Gitarre solo [1–3]
Very easy to intermediate-level pieces for guitar solo [1–4]
UE 33 667

Igel Gigels Gitarrenabenteuer 1
Spielstücke ab der frühen Begegnung mit der Gitarre [1–2] für Gitarre solo
Performance pieces for very early beginners for guitar solo [1–3]
UE 35 698

Igel Gigels Gitarrenabenteuer 2
Leichte Spielstücke für Gitarre solo [2]
Easy pieces for guitar solo [2–4]
UE 35 699

Béla Bartók
Für Kinder • For Children
bearbeitet für zwei Gitarren [2–3] • arranged for two guitars [2–5]
UE 37 209

Paul Coles

26 Melodic Studies
Leichte bis mittelschwere Etüden für Gitarre solo [1–3]
Easy to intermediate-level studies for guitar solo [1–4]
UE 21 670

From Folk to Classical 1
30 mittelschwere Bearbeitungen bekannter Stücke für Gitarre solo [2–3]
30 favourite pieces arranged for the middle-grade guitarist [3–4]
UE 21 673

Momentos Españoles
16 mittelschwere Stücke für Gitarre solo [3]
16 middle-grade solos [4–5]
UE 21 671

Dagda's Harp
Ein irisches Märchen für Gitarre solo [3–4]
An Irish Tale for guitar solo [6]
UE 21 672

---

* Schwierigkeitsgrad / Approximate gradings
[1–5] = Leicht – Fortgeschritten
[1–8] = Easy – Advanced